Rossendale

IN OLD PHOTOGRAPHS

The Maypole, Crawshaw Hall, 1912. The hall was built in 1830 and extended in 1869. Members of the Brooks family lived here for 145 years, their fortune coming from calico printing, quarrying, mining and landowning. (M. Sisley)

Rossendale

IN OLD PHOTOGRAPHS

BENITA MOORE ALA *and*
NICK DUNNACHIE

Sutton Publishing Limited
Phoenix Mill · Thrupp · Stroud
Gloucestershire · GL5 2BU

First Published 1994

Reprinted in 2002, 2004

Copyright © Benita Moore and
Nick Dunnachie, 1994

British Library Cataloguing in Publication Data.
A catalogue record for this book is available from
the British Library.

ISBN 0-7509-0783-5

Typeset in 9/10 Sabon.
Typesetting and origination by
Sutton Publishing Limited.
Printed in Great Britain by
J.H. Haynes & Co. Ltd, Sparkford.

Contents

Rossendale

R stands fer Rising Bridge
That's at Accrington end of t'vale.
O stands fer over t'moors
Where it blows a real gale.
S stands fer Stacksteads
Near Bacup and New Line.
Another **S** is ski slope
Which visitors vote fine.
E stands fer Edenfield
That's nicest place of all.
N stands fer Newchurch
With its churches standing tall.
D stands fer Deerplay
It were once an old coal mine.
A stands fer Acre
Where Winfields sell a good line.
L stands fer Loveclough
And also Lumb as well –
If you've enough money to live up theer
Then you must be quite a swell.
E stands fer everything
That's in this lovely vale,
And if yer owt like me
You'll be proud as can be
To live in ROSSENDALE.

Benita Moore ALA

6

Introduction

Rossendale is a beautiful borough, filled with green hills and valleys, rolling moors and rippling streams. Its hard-working people reflect the true Lancastrian spirit in their common bond of rural and industrial life which have existed side by side since the Industrial Revolution. Rossendale's boundaries start at Rising Bridge and end at Whitworth, some 13 miles distant, and encompass a variety of towns, villages and hamlets, each with their individual traditions and dialects, characters and people of note.

In the fourteenth century it is known that the Forest or Chase of Rossendale contained eleven vaccaries, or cattle pastures, and was poorly populated except for Haslingden, the only town of sufficient import to have a church. Deforestation was begun under an order of Henry VII, and with this began an expansion of both trade and population. The land being agriculturally poor, people turned for a livelihood to the domestic woollen industry which was firmly established by the sixteenth century. By the early nineteenth century the factory manufacture of woollens was the major industry, soon to be rivalled by the cotton industry. People flooded into the valley, drawn by the prospect of regular work and wages. However, this trade suffered because of the cotton famine of the 1860s and many cotton mills were taken over by the burgeoning slipper industry, which was to become one of the major sources of employment in Rossendale. With subsidiary industries such as box-making, quilting, rubber and chemical manufacture, there was a diversity of industry which led to the area becoming known as 'The Golden Valley'.

If industry was the gold, then the gems of the valley must be the people in it, and though the metal has worn away the jewels remain. It has to be admitted that many of the previous inhabitants of Rossendale were not of Lancastrian birth, but immigrants from other parts of the country. Having said that, their descendants, born and bred in Rossendale, take pride in their valley roots; roots so strong that many still live within hailing distance of their ancestors. True Rossendalians will understand perfectly the expression, 'If you flit two streets away, you become a foreigner.' So strong is this territorial pride, that it is with some trepidation, though mostly with pleasure, that through this book we venture to cross the invisible but definite boundaries to bring together glimpses of the industry, traditions and social activity which make up Rossendale, a truly Lancastrian borough.

Benita Moore and Nick Dunnachie

The total Holland's workforce, 1937. Walter Holland is in the centre of the front row.

The first Holland's van, purchased in 1927.

SECTION ONE

Rising Bridge, Haslingden, Helmshore and Edenfield

Stonefold village has changed considerably over the years. The factory, seen here in the background, has now gone and the village is far more rural, surrounded by fields and country cottages. A section of the track from Stonefold to Accrington formed part of the old King's Highway from Haslingden to Accrington.

St John's Walking Day, 1937. St John's, Stonefold, celebrated its centenary in 1986. Sadly, there are no longer any walking days, but from 1951 there was a Rose Queen. Frances Taylor, née Baxter, who still works at the school, was the first one.

St John's Walking Day, Blackburn Road, Acre, Haslingden, 1935. Present church members include May Tomlinson, who was enrolling member of the Stonefold Mothers' Union for a time, Laura Guest, a churchwarden and a member of the choir, and Alice Dickinson. The late Hilda Stanway, who died in 1994, was a prominent speaker at local church groups and wrote and recited many religious verses over the years.

An early 'Holland's Pie' van. The business began as a confectioner's shop in Lower Deardengate, Haslingden, in about 1851. By 1907, the bakery was moved to larger premises in John Street, Haslingden, where the Trades' Club now exists. In 1936 the company moved to its present premises on the border between Baxenden and Rising Bridge. Holland's pies were delivered by horse and cart until 1927 when the first delivery van was bought. Hot pies were taken to mills in the vicinity, much to the consternation of those bakers whose premises were close to the mills. By 1938 there were twenty Holland's vans making regular deliveries to chip shops around Lancashire. Pies were the most popular items, although cakes, sliced bread and jam sandwiches were also produced. Historically, people in the north-west eat more than double the average number of pies, Holland's being a firm favourite. (Lancashire County Council, Rossendale Library Service)

Marsden Square, Haslingden, was used for a variety of shows and public gatherings. This picture shows Fred Barlow senior receiving first prize at the May Day Horse Show, 30 April 1949. (C. & F. Barlow)

Maypole, Haslingden, outside the Empire cinema, Deardengate, c. 1906. Maypoles were very popular in Rossendale until the 1970s and '80s. Some children from local churches would dance round maypoles in the streets of Rossendale and then collect money for their local churches or charities. (C. & F. Barlow)

Haslingden Borough Band taking part in a united procession, *c.* 1955. Jim Haworth is playing baritone, third from right, second row. The photograph was taken in the schoolyard of Haslingden Secondary Modern School. (J. Haworth)

Bob (left) and Jim Haworth, stalwarts of Haslingden Borough Band, outside 'The Lindens', Market Place, Haslingden, 1930s. The Swan Hotel in the background has been demolished. (J. Haworth)

St James's Church procession in Manchester Road, Haslingden, *c.* 1910. The junction of Beaconsfield Street and Manchester Road is in the background. St James's Church, Haslingden, the 'top church' as it is known because of its prominent position overlooking the town, has been in existence for over 700 years, and still holds a traditional Walking Day around the town. The first recorded mention of Haslingden's parish church occurs at the time that the monks took possession of Whalley in 1284. The church is not mentioned in an earlier ecclesiastical document dated 1269, so it is fair to conclude that the church was founded between those dates, although it is possible that there was a church settlement in Haslingden at a much earlier date. The Chapelry of Haslingden formerly consisted of the townships of Haslingden, Henheads, Higher-Booths, Lower-Booths, and Dunnockshaw. As the population increased, other ecclesiastical districts were formed out of it. A church was established at Newchurch in 1511 and at Goodshaw in 1542, but it was not until 1850 that Goodshaw was made a separate chapelry. Edward VI granted an order compelling the inhabitants of Rawtenstall, Newhallhey, Gambleside, Loveclough, Crawshawbooth, Constable Booth, Oakenhead-wood Booth and Dunnockshaw Booth to attend divine service at Newchurch and fulfil all obligations thereto as parishioners. But as this order was met with disfavour, the inhabitants of the Booths were permitted to return legally to their original places of worship at Haslingden and its independent chapel of Goodshaw. (Lancashire County Council, Rossendale Library Service)

The Co-op, Deardengate, Haslingden, 1900. The largest of the many Co-op shops in the town, this one had millinery, drapery, furnishings, footwear and butchery departments. Meals for weddings and funerals were served upstairs in the hall, which was used for other purposes besides catering. In addition to selling everything a family could want, the Co-operative Society provided food for the spirit. In 1935/6, the Co-operative Society Educational Department hosted a variety of meetings. These included Lantern Lectures, 'Rambles in Spain', 'Shakespeare's Land', 'Stockholm – the Venice of the North', 'Russia and her Baltic Neighbours', 'Beauty Spots in Yorkshire', '5,000 miles with 1,000 Nazis' and 'The Brontë Country'. They also held grand concerts, with entertainment by 'The Scarlett Concert Party', 'The Sylvians', Tom Storey's 'Excelsiors' and the 'Xcels'. (Lancashire County Council, Rossendale Library Service)

The first meeting of Laneside Mothers' Union, *c.* 1900. There is a superb display of hats; feathers were popular for enhancing women's headgear and apparel in late Victorian and Edwardian times. (Lancashire County Council, Rossendale Library Service)

Parade for Colonel Hoyle's garden party, 12 July 1913. (Lancashire County Council, Rossendale Library Service)

Helmcroft, Helmshore Road. This scene was photographed in January 1940 during a bad winter, opposite where Haslingden Sports Centre now stands. (C. & F. Barlow)

Rose Queen, Musbury Church, officially St Thomas's Church, 1914. The Musbury Rose Queen tradition started before the First World War, then in about 1933 changed to Queen of the Seasons. The first of these was Dorothy Cranshaw, later Mrs Wise. Queen of the Seasons became Harvest Queen, and later still there was a revival of Rose Queens, one of these being Carolyn Wise, Dorothy's daughter. (C. & F. Barlow)

Mock wedding, St Thomas's Sunday School, Holcombe Road, Helmshore, 1930s. The bride was Maggie Metcalfe and the groom Tom Isherwood; guests included Arthur and Steven Waite, Alfred Whitaker, Albert Hugget, Dorothy Wise, Sarah Barlow, Tom Lambert, Bessie Edisford, Mary Ramsbottom, Frank Haslam, Mary Wise, S.A. Cooper, Hilda Wilkinson, Doris Cockshoot, Arthur Greenhow, Lizzie Edisford, Douglas Haslam, Mrs Waite, Mrs Woods and Mrs Barnes. Mock weddings were popular social events throughout the valley, and probably regionally. (C. & F. Barlow)

Coronation festivities at Helmshore, 1911. The mill chimney is connected by a long flue to the boilerhouse of the mill. Helmshore was mainly the creation of the Turner family, who were involved in the textile industry. The most prominent member was William Turner, an autocratic man who, using his position as a magistrate, once sentenced an employee to prison for 'spinning thick'. He was largely responsible for the erection of St Thomas's Church, which was consecrated on 25 March 1852. On the following day Turner's body was buried in the churchyard, his being the first grave to be dug there. The church has a peal of eight bells, each named after a daughter of William Turner. In 1902 the ringers were the first in Lancashire or the North of England ever to score a peal of London Surprise Major, 5,024 changes. (Lancashire County Council, Rossendale Library Service)

Co-op Row, Holcombe Road, Helmshore, 1911. Those pictured are celebrating the coronation of George V. (C. & F. Barlow)

An early Rose Queen festival, St Thomas's Church, Musbury, Helmshore. 1994 saw the 150th year of the forming of the parish of Musbury. This was celebrated with the crowning of the 1994 Festival Rose Queen, Francesca Doody, by Jean Warburton on 25 June. (C. & F. Barlow)

St Stephen's, Grane, Mothers' Union concert, 1965. Back row, left to right: Hannah Brown, Mrs Roundell, Mrs Greenwood, Mrs Rhona Keirs, Rose Howarth, Betty Hartley, Joan Baker, Mrs Fletcher. Middle row: Mrs Heywood, Eileen Nuttall, Eileen Proctor, Mrs A. Marsden, Maggy Bell. Front row: Mrs Barlow, Mrs Bamber, Nellie Cronshaw, Jean Baker, Eileen Gardner. Many of the functions arranged by the congregation and Mothers' Union were held in the Sunday School, originally known as the Mission. At the turn of the century a third reservoir was built in Grane and the majority of 'Graners' were moved from their homes because of the dangers of water pollution. Later, in the 1920s, St Stephen's Church, which once stood near the centre of Grane village, was dismantled stone by stone and rebuilt nearer to the centre of population. While this rebuilding was going on, services and ceremonies were held in the Mission, which had been built for that purpose. One romantic couple, wishing to be the first to be married in the newly re-opened church, went through the marriage ceremony and set off on their honeymoon. They found on their return that the licence to perform marriages had not been transferred from the Mission to the church, and as a result they were not married, an error which had to be put right by an Act of Parliament. (Garth Dawson)

Toll Bar, Ewood Bridge, 1950s. This was on the old road between Edenfield and Haslingden, near the New Bridge Inn. (H. O'Neill)

Lumb Old Hall. This is the oldest inhabited house in Rossendale. In 1298 the Rostherne (various spellings) family came here and stayed until about 1700. The hall then passed through various hands. Mrs Margaret Baldwin has been here since 1962. (Mrs M. Baldwin)

Village children at Irwell Vale dancing round the Maypole, 1993. Apparently the children from some local schools in the Rossendale area still do this in their own localities to help keep the tradition alive. (*Rossendale Free Press*)

The Pack Horse Inn, Edenfield, *c.* 1910. Left to right: Richard Nuttall and his sons, John Will, Jim and George. (Lancashire County Council, Rossendale Library Service)

Nuttall's cart, Edenfield, *c.* 1910. Richard Nuttall and Son's haulage business was founded by Richard and Jack Nuttall before the First World War, during which time they carried cloth from Rose Bowl Print Works to Manchester. Today the firm is run by old Dick's grandson – 'Young' Richard – and now carries paper from Trinity Paper Mill, Ramsbottom. (C. & F. Barlow)

Market Street, Edenfield, probably during a January in the early 1930s. In the terrible winter of that year Edenfield was cut off from Rochdale over the road via 'Owd Betts' for two weeks. Amos Taylor, an Edenfield resident, can remember walking on 5 ft of solid snow, and being able to open one of the street lamps. (Edenfield Local History Society)

Peace Celebrations at the Rostron's Arms, Edenfield, 1919. In the centre of the photograph, facing the camera, is Mrs Margaret Cort, mother of Elsie Whittaker – a well-known Edenfield resident. (Edenfield Local History Society)

Holcombe Brook to Edenfield Tram, taken at Guide Post, opposite Edenfield Church School, 1913. The man on the front step is Mr Wild; the man at the rear, wearing a trilby, is Bob Pilling; the lady with the floral hat is Mrs Richard Nuttall. (Edenfield Local History Society)

Market Place, Edenfield, *c.* 1928. To the right of the lamp stands Fisher's Restaurant, originally Gee's the bakers, now Sixsmith's Bakers. (J. Sixsmith)

Whit Walks, Market Street, Edenfield, 1920s. The various churches in Edenfield, Primitive Methodists, Wesleyan Methodists and the Parish Church, all held walking days throughout the year. (Edenfield Local History Society)

Class 6, Edenfield Church School, *c.* 1911. Mr Billy Greenwood was the headmaster at the time. At the turn of the century galleries such as the one shown were recommended by educationalists for the teaching of certain subjects. Amos Taylor attended the school from 1916 to 1925 and left at the age of fourteen. (Edenfield Local History Society)

SECTION TWO

Crawshawbooth, Goodshaw and Loveclough

Picture postcard of Crawshawbooth, *c.* 1910, showing Crawshaw Hall, Goodshaw Church, Wesleyan Church, Friends' Meeting House and St John's Church (centre). (C. & F. Barlow)

St John's Church, Crawshawbooth, 1986. (E. Birchall)

Friends' Meeting House, Crawshawbooth, *c.* 1979. (E. Birchall)

Shepherds' Club Procession, Crawshawbooth, taken outside the mill at Dunnockshaw, 15 September 1926. (H. O'Neill)

Crawshawbooth centre, 1986. (E. Birchall)

This is presumed to be pig baiting, early twentieth century. There have been instances of bull baiting and badger baiting in the valley but, as far as we know, this is the first time that pig baiting has been brought to the attention of the public. It is difficult to believe that a thrifty Rossendale farmer would risk losing a beast that hadn't yet grown to marketable size. (H. O'Neill)

Crankshaw's, Burnley Road, Crawshawbooth, thought to be opposite the Dog Inn, c. 1905. The girl in the doorway appears to be wearing some of the vegetables on her hat. Recently the council have been clamping down on shopkeepers who break the by-laws by stacking their goods on the pavement outside their shops. (H. O'Neill)

Compston's Cross, located on the moors behind Clowbridge Reservoir, from which position wonderful views of the valley can be enjoyed. Samuel Compston was a local writer and historian, and an ex-mayor of Rawtenstall; he erected the cross in 1902, near the site of two ancient crosses. (E. Birchall)

Tom Fort's Fish, Chip and Tripe Saloon, also licensed to sell tobacco and cigars, *c.* 1905. (H. O'Neill)

Goodshaw Band giving a winning performance at Rochdale in 1946, their first contest after the war. (J. Haworth)

Goodshaw Band showing off their new uniforms in Whitaker Park, 1953. (J. Haworth)

Goodshaw Fold, *c.* 1906. (H. O'Neill)

Goodshaw Youth Club Football Team, 1960. Sitting centre front is Ian Spencer, captain. (H. O'Neill)

Clowbridge Reservoir under construction, 1890. (H. O'Neill)

The late Mrs Mary Robinson was a well-known Crawshawbooth character who was often seen walking her dogs round the village. She helped many local charities and actually collapsed and died while opening a fête when she was over eighty years old. (E. Birchall)

Holcombe Hunt at Loveclough, *c.* 1980. (E. Birchall)

SECTION THREE

Rawtenstall

Bank Street, Rawtenstall, pre-1909, before the electrification of the trams. (Lancashire County Council, Rossendale Library Service)

Thorn Hill, Haslingden Old Road, early 1900s. The 'taking-in' steps of the weavers' cottages can be seen. The pub at the bottom of the hill is the Bishop Blaize, recently renamed Madison Park Wine Lodge. (H. O'Neill)

The Old Astoria, billing Ivy Benson and her all-girls orchestra, 1940s. Many of the big bands appeared at the Astoria, which was a popular venue for dancers throughout Lancashire. The shoe shop window on the left was once a show window for Myerscough's cars. St Mary's Church tower is in the background. (Lancashire County Council, Rossendale Library Service)

The old bus station, with the library and St Mary's Church in the background, 1950s. The library, still one of the finest buildings in Rawtenstall, first opened its doors in June 1906. A year later it was officially opened by Andrew Carnegie, who had donated the library to the borough, accompanied by Lewis Harcourt MP and members of the town council. The photograph was taken from a point close to where the new fire station now stands. The block of property in this area was known as Cheapside. (Lancashire County Council, Rossendale Library Service)

St Mary's Church before the tower was rebuilt in the 1880s. On the left can be seen the roof of the old school. (H. O'Neill)

Woodtop Mission Procession on Bury Road, passing by A. Haworth's, bakery and confectionery, c. 1930. (H. O'Neill)

The 'Bluebirds' on Walking Day, at the bottom of Grange Road. The 'Bluebirds' were young Conservatives and belonged to the Conservative Club, visible in the background.

Springside Jubilee Methodists' Walking Day, late 1940s. This photograph was taken from Newchurch Road looking down towards the market, showing the bottom half of Crankshaw Street.

Cattle markets were held on vacant land adjacent to Burnley Road. However, this photograph, *c*. 1900, is more likely to be a cattle fair, being held opposite St James-the-Less, on the site of Hobson Street and Alexandria Street. Cattle fairs were originally held on Tup Meadow. (Lancashire County Council, Rossendale Library Service)

Night wagon, 1902. The Environmental Health Service was the oldest of Rawtenstall's services. In 1891 there was no main sewerage scheme, streets were unpaved, pails, privies and insanitary ashpits abounded and their contents were discharged on the land. In 1897 houses were connected to the new sewerage system which was started in 1894, and in 1907 the Rawtenstall Corporation Act required the conversion of pail and privy closets in the borough. (Lancashire County Council, Rossendale Library Service)

Tramlines being laid at Lockgate, Haslingden Road, *c.* 1908. (Lancashire County Council, Rossendale Library Service)

Horse-drawn buses owned by Roberts and Co. operated a service between Rawtenstall and Burnley, *c.* 1900. (Lancashire County Council, Rossendale Library Service)

Old steam trams, part of the Baltic fleet, being broken up for scrap. They were replaced by electric trams, *c*. 1909. (H. O'Neill)

Tram breaking on the site of the old tram shed, 15 May 1909, the day the trams were electrified in Rawtenstall. (H. O'Neill)

The Ram's Head public house on Newchurch Road, seen from the top of Bank Street, 1920s. (H. O'Neill)

Steam wagon belonging to Ben Barnes and Sons, Carriers, 1920s. Their headquarters used to be at Cheapside on Haslingden Road, but are now based at Holly Mount, the mansion which belonged to the Whitehead family. The modern wagons of Ben Barnes & Sons Ltd, are as familiar a sight on Rossendale roads as the vans of Holland's Pies. (H. O'Neill)

Rawtenstall's old fire station was replaced by a new one which stands in the middle of the town's biggest roundabout, *c.* 1910. Before 1934 street lighting in Rawtenstall was under the control of the superintendent of the local fire brigade. In 1891 the Borough of Rawtenstall was lit entirely by gas; the first electric lamps were installed about 1912, and at least some of these early lamps were of the carbon arc type. By 1934, the change-over from gas to electricity was virtually complete; the last route to be lit by gas in the borough was Cowpe Road. (Lancashire County Council, Rossendale Library Service)

Rawtenstall Market, 1956. The first indoor market in Rawtenstall was built in 1905 and extended in 1912. The original Market Hall burnt down in 1946, the fire caused by the backfiring of a motorcycle in one of the shops forming part of the original building, where the open market now stands. (Lancashire County Council, Rossendale Library Service)

Rawtenstall Open Market, with the roof of the Market Hall behind, 1994. The scene has changed little over the years. (B. Moore)

Inside Rawtenstall Market Hall, 1994. (B. Moore)

Vi Holmes on Lord's Tripe Stall, Rawtenstall Market, 1990s. Lord's tripe was part of Rossendale from the early 1900s when Thomas Lord had a small tripe works at Waterfoot. His only daughter, later Mrs Mary Marlow, carried on the business for many years and, indeed, still serves on the tripe stall on most market days. The business has now changed hands, but Mary still takes a lively interest in it. (B. Moore)

Ken Duxbury's general stall, Open Market, Rawtenstall, 1994. (B. Moore)

Gladys Hunt's book stall, Rawtenstall Market, 1949. (D. Hunt)

Dinah Hunt's book stall, Rawtenstall Market, 1994. Dinah is the daughter-in-law of Gladys Hunt and took over from her over thirty years ago. (B. Moore)

Walter Brown's shop, 99 Bank Street, where tea was advertised at a shilling a pound, *c.* 1910. Nowadays you can't buy a single cup of tea for that price. The premises are now occupied by Manning's confectioners. (Lancashire County Council, Rossendale Library Service)

Herbal Health Shop, Bank Street, 1980s. A fascinating range of tonics and remedies are sold at one of the country's few remaining temperance bars. (H. O'Neill)

SECTION FOUR

Cloughfold, Water, Newchurch, Lumb, Waterfoot and Whitewell Bottom

Donkey stoning the steps, *c.* 1961. This was a weekly MUST for every proud Lancashire housewife for many years. In point of fact, many of Rossendale's pensioners still continue this historic tradition as a matter of housewifely pride. (E. Birchall)

Hareholme Methodist Walking Day, *c.* 1930. Mrs Emma Edge, wife of Fred Edge, the Waterfoot blacksmith, attended here for many years, and was a Sunday school teacher and superintendent for a period. The church closed in the 1960s. (C. Spencer)

Cloughfold, 1960s. The Rossendale Union Gas Co. was formed in 1854. The signals were for Cloughfold station. (H. O'Neill)

Cloughfold celebrations for the Diamond Jubilee of Queen Victoria, 1897. This photograph was taken on Bacup Road between Rawtenstall and Waterfoot. (Lancashire County Council, Rossendale Library Service)

Higher Cloughfold, from Dobbin Lane, *c.* 1910. The horse is outside the Red Lion; the house is Spring Hill, now a nursing home. The building on the left is Lodge Fold Farm; the left-hand road goes to Rawtenstall, the right-hand one to Newchurch. (Lancashire County Council, Rossendale Library Service)

A panoramic view of Newchurch with St Nicholas' Church in the background, 1980s. (H. O'Neill)

York Street, Newchurch, 1950s. (H. O'Neill)

Crumpet seller on Old Street, Newchurch, *c.* 1910. (Lancashire County Council, Rossendale Library Service)

Old Street, Newchurch, *c.* 1920. Taken before the new bungalows were built, the photograph shows a weaver's cottage with exterior steps leading up to the loomshop. The steps are railed on one side only to make it easier for a worker to carry the beam full of warp. The textile industry had a great impact on the types of dwellings throughout Rossendale, ranging from weavers' cottages and terraced housing for factory operatives to mansions for the mill owners. (H. O'Neill)

Harrison's milk float at Newchurch, *c.* 1912. 'Families supplied twice daily' was their boast. (H. O'Neill)

Church Street, Newchurch, *c.* 1910. The pub in the left foreground is the Boar's Head. (H. O'Neill)

Waterfoot Sunday schools demonstration, *c.* 1902. This photograph was taken outside Trickett's Arcade, built by Sir H.W. Trickett, the 'Slipper King'. As a boy he worked in a felt manufacturers and rose to become a leading light in Rossendale, being five times mayor of Rawtenstall and knighted for his services to industry. (H. O'Neill)

Syd Smith, a local boxer, at Waugh's Well, on the moors above Waterfoot, a favourite walk, especially at Whitsuntide and Easter. A farmhouse nearby supplied thirsty ramblers with tea. In July an annual pilgrimage is made by fans of the renowned Lancashire dialect poet Edwin Waugh to perpetuate his memory. (S. Smith)

Dick Ireland, the 'black pudding man' of Waterfoot, 1989. If you don't know what goes into a black pudding, don't ask, just enjoy the taste. (B. Moore)

The closing room at Gaghills Slipper Works, Waterfoot, 1920s, owned by Sir H.W. Trickett who made his fortune in the footwear industry, and was the first man to sell slippers by mail order. (Lambert Haworth PLC)

Ivy Cottages, Townsend Street, Waterfoot, 1920s. The roof of the Bacup and Rawtenstall Grammar School can be seen in the background. The pupils went for swimming lessons at Bacup baths, travelling there by train. Around 1930, while passing through the tunnel, one boy seeking revenge on another, leapt on him in the darkness, only to find on leaving the tunnel that his hands were gripping the neck of a lady traveller. (H. O'Neill)

Cowpe Reservoir, 1910. Water has played an important part in the development of Rossendale's textile industry, powering fulling mills, and later weaving sheds. A number of reservoirs were constructed in the nineteenth century, using Irish labourers who did not always get on well with the natives. It has been suggested that the field walls in some areas of Rossendale were filled with gold sovereigns, the argument being that when the local mill workers had been paid, the Irish labourers would challenge them to fight for their wages. To protect their earnings, the cautious operatives would hide their wages, which included a sovereign, in a convenient wall, but forget where they had secreted their money. Another unlikely story. (H. O'Neill)

Rawtenstall Corporation bus outside Bridge End House, Waterfoot (now used as a library and neighbourhood office), late 1920s. The house at one time belonged to Mr Lupton, a former billiard hall owner and mayor of Rawtenstall who was elected in 1945. (H. O'Neill)

The Glen, Waterfoot, also known as 'The Thrutch', mid-1920s. This chimney belongs to Baxter's Glen Top Brewery, but the site is now just a garden. The tunnel, now closed, made it possible for the train to go to Bacup. The brewery was owned by John Baxter, who lived in a large house nearby which is still standing. His brother, William H., was proprietor of Lower Lane Brewery, Haslingden, and was mayor of Haslingden. (Lancashire County Council, Rossendale Library Service)

Burnley Road East, Waterfoot, taken from Mill End looking towards Waterfoot in the early 1900s. The taller building in the distance is the Bethel Baptist Chapel, a once thriving church which sadly closed its doors in 1994.

Burnley Road, Waterfoot, 1880. The tower of St Nicholas's Church, Newchurch, is visible on the left. (H. O'Neill)

The centre of Waterfoot looking towards Bacup, *c.* 1915. The horse and cart are outside the Royal Hotel. A house in the block on the left is known as 'Dental Villa' because it has been in continuous use as a dentist's since it was built in 1895. John Maden, the first dentist there, extracted teeth (without pain) using nitrous oxide, and sold sets of teeth from a guinea upwards. (Photograph courtesy H. O'Neill)

Waterfoot Sunday schools demonstration in Burnley Road East, *c.* 1905. The Mason's Arms is on the right. (H. O'Neill)

Cowpe village, stretching up towards Kearns Mill. (H. O'Neill)

Greenbridge Mill, at the bottom of Cowpe Road, Waterfoot, *c.* 1920. This mill burned down and another of the same name was built in Rawtenstall. (H. O'Neill)

Burnley Road, Scoutbottom, early 1960s. (H. O'Neill)

A similar, but earlier, view of Burnley Road, *c.* 1910. (H. O'Neill)

Lambert Howarth's Rossendale Mill at Whitewell Bottom. Taken in 1935, the photograph shows the Christmas decorations in the closing room before the installation of a belt conveyor system. (Lambert Howarth PLC)

Mary Chadwick, daughter of the famous Bury Black Pudding firm, preparing the mixture at her little factory in Whitewell Bottom. (B. Moore)

Windle's Sweets, Whitewell Bottom, 1920s. Their slogan was: 'Superior boiled sugars in large variety'. (H. O'Neill)

Water Band, *c.* 1935. The band is well known, not only in Rossendale but all over the north of England where it has taken part in many competitions and won a number of trophies. The band was formed in 1866 and still holds its meetings in the Band Room adjacent to the Lumb Baptist chapel. Donald Barker, who procured this photograph, joined the band in 1920 and still helps in many ways. (C. Brown)

Chip shop, Water, *c.* 1920. (H. O'Neill)

Eden Methodist Chapel, Burnley Road East, Lumb. This was opened in 1874 and the congregation have just celebrated their hundred-and-twentieth anniversary. One of the stalwarts of the chapel is Mrs Emma Hunt, who first attended when she was eight years old, and is now over seventy. Other long-serving members of the congregation include James Allen, Henry Howarth and Harry Collins. (E. Haworth)

Eden Chapel Whit Walk, *c.* 1920. Harry Baldwin, Ted Hornby, Tommy Jeffrey and Sam Hunt are among those pictured here. (E. Hunt)

The tram to Water, taken during a stop at Lumb, 1911. (H. O'Neill)

Lumb valley. The houses on the left, known as Lumb Bank, are now demolished. The electric tram indicates that the photo was taken after 1911. (H. O'Neill)

Lumb Valley Print Works: Mitchell, Ashworth and Stansfield's Albert Mill, a felt works, c. 1900. Rossendale once had a thriving felt industry. Block printers wrapped pieces of felt round their feet, a practice which ultimately led to the development of the slipper industry. (H. O'Neill)

Forest Holme, Lumb, taken looking towards Rawtenstall, c. 1900. (H. O'Neill)

Lumb Baptist church, looking towards Water, 1910. (H. O'Neill)

Hargreaves Arms, Lumb – a favourite 'eating-out' place, 1910. (H. O'Neill)

Farmer's milk float, Lumb, *c*. 1915. (H. O'Neill)

The Hargreaves Arms and Lumb parish church, *c*. 1910.

Lumb parish church, *c.* 1910. St Michael's Church was built between 1847 and 1848 by J. Clarke at a cost of £2,060.

Water County Primary School, 1940s. The new building was erected in 1895. Water CP School has a famous choir which represented England for the best choir in 'McDonald's Child of Achievement, Music in the Community', in 1992.

SECTION FIVE

Stacksteads

Newchurch Road, Stacksteads, looking towards Waterfoot, *c*. 1910. The lady on the left is in the doorway of the Commercial Hotel; next door is the Railway Hotel, and the tall building is Beaconsfield Conservative Club. The houses on the right have been demolished. (H. O'Neill)

Atherton Holme Mill, Stacksteads, *c.* 1970. The mill is still in use. The route of the railway can also be seen. (H. O'Neill)

Firemen, Farholme Mill, Stacksteads, *c.* 1890, now Valley Supply. (H. O'Neill)

Waterbarn Mill chimney, looking towards Stacksteads. The track was the route of the railway. Holy Trinity Church, Tunstead, can be seen in the background. Between 1934 and 1968 the mill was used for the production of jams, mineral water and confectionery. (H. O'Neill)

Duckworth's grocery shop, Stacksteads, 1910. This shop stood at the bottom of Toll Bar. Note the hoist on the gable end of the building. (H. O'Neill)

The Bacup Co-op Stores Ltd, Stacksteads, at the top of Branch Street, 1930s. It was used as a launderette in this century before it was demolished. Bacup was one of the first towns to develop a co-operative system, following the example of Rochdale, pioneers of the movement. (H. O'Neill)

Herbert Hacking & Son, Stacksteads. This monumental mason's business in Stacksteads was run by Herbert's father. The row of houses in the background is Prospect Terrace.

Newchurch Road, Stacksteads, *c.* 1906. All the houses on the left-hand side have now gone, to be replaced by a car-park. The Rose and Bowl Restaurant is on the right-hand side. (H. O'Neill)

Baxter's Brewery horse, *c.* 1910. Note that the horse's tail has been shaved for hygiene. The photograph was taken at Blackwood, near the Railway public house. Blackwood used to be a thriving little community with its own pub and shops. (H. O'Neill)

St Luke's Mission, Holme Street, Stacksteads, 1950s. (H. O'Neill)

Beulah Methodist church, Britannia. This photograph was taken in 1935, the church's golden jubilee year. (Lancashire County Council, Rossendale Library Service)

Acre Mill Baptist Sunday school, 1889. Acre Mill church is still going strong. (H. O'Neill)

Tunstead C. of E. Walking Day, *c.* 1928. The procession is coming down Booth Road, with Plantation Street and Chapel Street to the left. (J. Foden)

Waterbarn Chapel. This is an early view of the interior, which was later modernized. Note the extensive stencilling. The chapel is now up for sale. Sir H.W. Trickett is buried in the graveyard. (H. O'Neill)

Outing from the Beehive Inn, Waterbarn, Newchurch Road, Stacksteads, *c.* 1915. The sign on the charabanc indicates that it was limited to travel at 12 mph. A charabanc would serve as a wagon during the week, but at weekends the vehicle would have a passenger body attached to it, and then be used for outings. Some would have a hood stored in a compartment at the back of the vehicle. During inclement weather the hood would be unfolded, the passengers passing it over their heads to the front. With no windows on the sides, the passengers would still be affected by the elements. (H. O'Neill)

The Home Guard, Stacksteads, 1940s. Those are possibly Lee quarries in the background. (S. Smith)

Rochdale Road, Britannia, post-electrification of the trams, *c*. 1912. (H. O'Neill)

Bacup Coconutters at Rawtenstall, *c*. 1972. (E. Birchall)

Bacup Coconutters at New Line, Bacup, 1980s. (H. O'Neill)

Bacup, Weir and Sharneyford

Bacup, before 1903. Todmorden Road is visible on the left. Note the close proximity of the three factory chimneys, unusual even in Rossendale.

Cattle being taken to the butchers. This photograph was taken at the top of Union Street, outside the Yorkshire Bank, in the early 1900s. One of the men is Bill Hollows from Stacksteads.

Bacup Sunday school procession, 1902. The view is of Burnley Road; the River Irwell is on the other side of the low wall, as yet unculverted. (H. O'Neill)

Burnley Road, Bacup, 1890. Burnley Road leads into the centre of Bacup. Seen here are the Bull's Head Hotel and bridge, with Boston Street on the left. (H. O'Neill)

Old Angel Hotel, *c.* 1900, on the site of the former Woolworths – now a video shop – at the bottom of Lane Head Lane. Mary A. Shepherd was the 'Licensed Retailer of Wines, Spirits, Ales and Porters'. Engraved on the lower windows are the words 'Smoke Room' and 'Commercial Room'. (H. O'Neill)

Bacup skating rink in the early 1900s before being converted to the Gem cinema. There was also a skating rink in Herbert Street, Stacksteads. (H. O'Neill)

Crippled children's treat. Taken during the First World War, this photograph shows the convoy coming down Burnley Road, Bacup. (H. O'Neill)

Coronation decorations, St James's Street, Bacup, 22 June 1911. The Mechanics' Institute, now the library, is in the background. (H. O'Neill)

St John's Church and War Memorial, Bacup, 1923.

Bridge Street, Bacup, *c.* 1908. Freeman, Hardy and Willis's shop is on the left.

Market Street, Bacup, at the junction of Bankside Lane, *c.* 1910. The property on the right was part of an island block which has been demolished.

The footwear department of the old Co-op, Union Street, Bacup, selling clogs, boots and shoes in the early 1900s.

Weaving shed, Olive Mill, Bacup, *c.* 1901. The absence of belt drives from overhead shafting indicates that the factory was powered by electricity. The lady on the right is Clara Smith.

Parrock Mill's Christmas party, *c.* 1936. The festivities took place at the Liberal Club, Burnley Road, Bacup.

Old lady at her fireside, Bacup. The fire-range had a number of uses: cooking, heating water and warming the room. In earlier years, the cloth on the mantelpiece would often have crocheted tassels hanging down, inside which were glass balls taken from old-fashioned bottles.

Bacup Central School, 1914.

Sharneyford School, 1930s. Sharneyford is situated on the Todmorden Road up above Bacup, and is one of the last outposts of Rossendale.

Rag and bone man – 'Happy Jack' John Whitehead of Lanehead Lane, who died in 1939 – seen here in a Bacup street. He used a football rattle to announce his presence. (H. O'Neill)

Old paraffin wagon, taken at Dog Pits, Burnley Road. To either side of the boy, taps can be seen jutting from the side of the cart. T. Smith, Bacup, was born in 1889, and died in 1967. The humans are as well shod as the horse.

Possibly an outing from St Saviour's Church, on Park Road, Bacup, 1904. Twenty-one passengers are already on board, three more are waiting, and there are two horses to do the work.

Butcher's van of Ormerod Mitchell, advertising 'English beef' and 'Scotch mutton', c. 1920.

Old Outdoor Market, Bacup. The land for the market ground and Market Hall was purchased in 1867, and a further piece of land was acquired for a drapery market, commonly known as the 'Rag Market'. The Market Hall, which appears on the right, was completed in 1867 and was referred to as a 'commodious building, in the Italian style of architecture'. Like so many others, Bacup Market suffered a loss of trade during the Second World War, and the open market was transferred to its present site at Temple Court. Despite a petition organized by the Market Hall traders, the building was closed in 1956. (Lancashire County Council, Rossendale Library Service)

Old Outdoor Market at the turn of the century. The building behind is the Market Hall. The woman on the right is standing outside Bacup Police Station, which was seen many times in the television series 'Juliet Bravo'.

Bacup Market Centenary, 1967. (Lancashire County Council, Rossendale Library Service)

Outdoor Market, Bacup, 1994. (B. Moore)

Carter's fruit stall, Bacup Market. (B. Moore)

Irwell Springs Printing Co. wagons, *c.* 1920.

Irwell Springs band at the opening of an event put on by the CWS, probably late 1920s or early '30s.

The old Doals chapel, Weir.

A general view of Weir with Burnley Road in the background.

The Weir Hotel, Weir, *c.* 1920. Adverts on the wall are for Sunlight soap and Lyon's tea.

Taken outside the Co-op shop branch No. 1, Weir, *c.* 1910. The legend on the cart reads 'John Rushton & Sons, Slaters, Lee Mill, Bacup'.

Broadclough Mill, Bacup. These dyeworks were connected with the Whitehead family. The original building, built in 1790, was designed by John Sutcliffe of Halifax.

Rookery Nook, Broadclough, Bacup, *c.* 1910.

Deerplay Inn, Bacup, in the early 1900s, sold ales and beers supplied by Grimshaw's Brewery, Burnley.

Irwell Inn, Burnley Road, Bacup, 1984.

Steam-powered wagon of Temperley & Sons Ltd, pottery manufacturers of Sharneyford, Bacup, *c.* 1900. The company's motto at carnival time was 'We Drain the World'.

A more unusual horse-drawn vehicle, taken near the New Inn, Rochdale Road, Bacup, *c.* 1900.

Shawforth, Facit and Whitworth

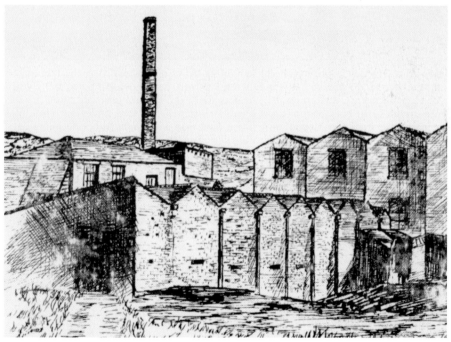

Freeholds Mill, Shawforth – a drawing by J.E. Newble, reproduced by kind permission of his niece.

Mary Alice Hartley, more familiarly known as 'Ailse o' Fusser's' was the last of the 'lime-gal' drivers. She made her way to Rochdale from her Shawforth home many years ago. Her appearance was grotesque; she was short and fat and over her petticoats she wore a man's top coat. A Jim-crow hat was fastened and tied under her chin. She carried a long stick and looked more like a man than a woman. In her declining days Ailse lived at Potovens, a cottage on the edge of the moor above Shawforth, but still used a donkey to carry coal for her customers. This donkey, Jerry, was her great favourite. He even shared her home, being tied to the bedpost at night. When Ailse died she was buried in Whitworth churchyard, a short distance from the pack-horse road she had often travelled. Jerry was sold to a local farmer and Ailse's lime-gal bell went to a Bacup doctor. There was a time when as many as twenty gals carried bags of coal from Land Coal Pit, near Shawforth, and sometimes lime from Clitheroe or Burnley. They travelled the pack-horse roads from Clitheroe to Bacup on the moors skirting Shawforth and Whitworth along the foot of Brown Wardle, down Cronkeyshaw to Rochdale. (Lancashire County Council, Rossendale Library Service)

Millgate Baptist Church by J.E. Newble, reproduced by kind permission of his niece.

Shawforth Methodist Procession, taken at the 'Top of the Shore', 10 June 1962.
(Lancashire County Council, Rossendale Library Service)

Station Road, Facit, with Westville in the background at the turn of the century. There is substantial evidence of horse-drawn vehicles having recently been in the street. (Lancashire County Council, Rossendale Library Service)

Church Street, Whitworth, *c.* 1910. (Lancashire County Council, Rossendale Library Service)

Cheetham Hill, Facit, *c.* 1910. (Lancashire County Council, Rossendale Library Service)

The Whitworth doctors' house. The Taylors were a famous medical family who practised for over 150 years and produced no less than twenty-six doctors in six generations, most of whom practised in Whitworth at one time or another. The first of the family to settle in the town was James Taylor, a farrier, who came from Bacup. His son, also called James, carried on the trade but developed an interest in horse ailments, particularly broken or malformed bones and cancers. These problems being common to horses and humans, it was not long before James was treating both, thus starting a medical tradition in the family which was to bring them fame and prosperity. From contemporary accounts, it would appear that the treatment offered by the Whitworth doctors differed from that given by other practitioners: 'They made no gradual and insidious advances on disease, but opened against it a bombardment of shot and shell from all directions. They bled their patients by the gallon, and drugged them by the stone. Their druggists, Ewbank and Wallis of York, used to supply them with a ton of Glaubers' salts at a time. Every Sunday morning they bled gratis anyone who liked to demand a prick from their lancets. Often, a hundred people were seated on the surgery benches at the same time, waiting venesection. When each of the party had found a seat, the two brothers passed rapidly along the line of bared arms, the one doctor deftly applying the ligature above the elbow, and the other immediately opening the vein, the crimson stream from which was directed into a wooden trough that ran round the apartment in which the operations were performed.' (Lancashire County Council, Rossendale Library Service)

Whitworth Carnival, 30 July 1910. Rushcart and Morris dancers from St Bartholomew's Church, facing the Dog and Partridge. The tradition of the Whitworth rushcart and rushbearing ceremony is still held every year in early September. The opinion most generally held is that rushbearing sprang from the recommendation of Pope Gregory IV to the early priesthood, that on the anniversary of the formation of their churches the priest should cover the floor with rushes and solemnize the day with sober festivity. (Lancashire County Council, Rossendale Library Service)

Whitworth Carnival, outside the Bar Garage, Market Street, *c.* 1951. (Lancashire County Council, Rossendale Library Service)

Whitworth Festival, outside Brookside Mill, 1920s. The theme of the display was 'ancient and modern' – now all of it looks quite ancient. (Lancashire County Council, Rossendale Library Service)

Whitworth Carnival, 1951, with Coconutters. (Lancashire County Council, Rossendale Library Service)

Bacup Coconutters in the Square, Whitworth Festival 1971. There are two Red Lions in Whitworth; this one is in the Square, close to the residence of the Whitworth doctors. The Whitworth Morris Men are different: Morris Men do not blacken their faces, wear white shirts instead of black and have a different form of headgear. (Lancashire County Council, Rossendale Library Service)

Whitworth Festival, 1964. Originally it was known as the festival, later became the carnival and then reverted to being the festival again. (Lancashire County Council, Rossendale Library Service)

Whitworth Old People's Welfare Party, 12 January 1957. (Lancashire County Council, Rossendale Library Service)

Women's Unionist Association Coffee Morning, Whitworth, 1 December 1962. Left to right: Mrs E. Lake, Mrs A. Jackson, Mrs V. Dodson, Mrs C. Holt, Mrs M. Pearson, Mrs Tony Leavy, Mrs S. Mitchell. (Lancashire County Council, Rossendale Library Service)

First inspection of the tram track on Hall Street, Whitworth, *c.* 1910. 'Bury, Rochdale and Oldham Tramway Company completed a tramline along the turnpike road to Facit, and this was a great facility to the workpeople, as well as to the inhabitants visiting Rochdale. In 1891, unfortunately, a dispute arose between the Whitworth Local Board and the Tram Company as to the repairs in the road, and we regret to state that in September of that year trams discontinued running. At the present time (1897) the tramcars ran from Rochdale to Healey.' (From William Robertson's *Rochdale and the Vale of Whitworth*)

In Loving Memory of the

Whit'oth Motor Bus,

Which fell asleep on Saturday, June 30th, 1906,

At Huntingdon,

AGED 2 DAYS AND 4 HOURS;

And was respectfully interred by sorrowing relatives at Leicester, July 1st.

An enigmatic reference to a Whitworth bus which appears not to have seen long service. (Lancashire County Council, Rossendale Library Service)

Park Green, Whitworth, 1954. The bowling green still offers popular and well-attended social events. (Lancashire County Council, Rossendale Library Service)

Healey Dell viaduct can still be viewed in the Healey Dell Nature Reserve, which provides a fascinating network of walks in a superb countryside setting. The railway viaduct stands 150 ft above the bed of the River Spodden; built of local stone, it has eight arches, each of 30 ft span. It opened in 1870 at a cost of £100,000. (Lancashire County Council, Rossendale Library Service)

Acknowledgements

The authors would like to thank the following people and institutions for the loan of photographs, and for help with information in compiling the text. Many of the photographs come from Rossendale Library Service, Lancashire County Council, and individual collections. We are grateful for the help given and the loan of material.

Special thanks to Susan Halstead, Valerie Spencer and Victor Marcinkiewitz of the Library Service, Carol and Fred Barlow, Eric Birchall ARPS, Harry O'Neill, Mrs M. Disley and Walter Holland and Son Ltd for their time and co-operation. Thanks are also due to the *Rossendale Free Press*, Bacup Natural History Society, Edenfield Local History Society, Kathy Fishwick of Rawtenstall Civic Society, Sandra Cruise of Rossendale Museum, and Wilfred and Kathleen Foulds.